The Visitation to Athelhampton Hall

Published in 2021 by Athelhampton House, Athelhampton,
Dorchester, Dorset, DT2 7LG

Tel:- 01305 848363
Email:- hello@athelhampton.co.uk
Web:- www.athelhampton.co.uk

Designed by Owen Davies

ISBN number: 978-0-9555815-3-3

In the spring of 1996, I visited Athelhampton for the very first time. I had just joined the small team here looking after the numerous visitors, day-trippers and tourists who would make their way to visit the fine Tudor Manor house and its gardens, which had just won the prestigious 'Garden of the Year' award, some 100 years after they were created by the then owner Alfred Cart de Lafontaine and his garden architect Francis Inigo Thomas.

Athelhampton has a varied history, through generations the house has gently swayed between a prosperous family home and a forgotten relic of the past. In 1891, after years of one such decline, It was purchased by a young gentleman, Alfred Cart de Lafontaine. Over a few years he restored the house, in part to its Tudor heritage but also to his taste and needs, including the library, the green parlour and the arts & crafts style formal gardens.

His wealth allowed the importation of thousands of tonnes of Ham Stone from Somerset to create the garden structure we see today. He created luxurious rooms within the house and added a collection of antiquities that seem better suited to a museum, but 25 years later, after he suffered a personal tragedy he suddenly sold Athelhampton and his collection.

For a man who left such a mark on a singular place, he has become somewhat of an enigma. If we look to find out more about him, despite extensive enquiries and research, we find he is almost untraceable, barely leaving another record of his existence.

Though he appeared somewhat reluctant, in 1899 he gave a tour to the Dorchester Field Club, His tour and talk, written up in our archive, gives us today an opportunity to explore the manor house with him, almost listening to his voice, offering a rare insight into his world at Athelhampton.

Owen Davies
Estate Manager

The House Tour

starting under the Cedar Tree

1899

I have been asked by our excellent Honorary Secretary to give you some account of this house and its many points of interest. To this request I very reluctantly consented, for I cannot but feel that there are many present who are better qualified than myself to speak on the architectural beauties of Athelhampton and its history, both from a greater knowledge of the period, and also, most certainly, from a longer acquaintance with the place.

However, with your kind indulgence, I will do my best, prefacing my remarks with the assurance of the great pleasure it gives me to welcome the Dorset Field Club here to-day.

The origin of the name Athelhampton, or more correctly Athelhampstan, is somewhat uncertain. Coker, in his "Survey of Dorsetshire", says "the veri name intimates nobilitie," and thus, even though the old tradition of its being King Athelstan's residence be thrown overboard, there remain the three Saxon words - ATHEL (noble), HAM (habitation), and STAN (denoting the superlative degree) to intimate a sufficient degree of eminence. Hutchins thinks it probable that Athelhelme, one of the Saxon earls of Dorset, gave name to the place. He is styled a "duke" or general (dux) in the Saxon Chronicles: and in 837 he commanded the Dorsetshire men in an engagement at Portland with Dates, in which he lost his life.

In the time of Richard II, the estate was in the possession of two families named respectively de Londres and de Pydele, whose arms you will find in the east and west windows of the great hall. From these families Athelhampton descended by marriage to the very ancient family of Martin, or Fitz-Martyn, about the middle of the 14th century. Martin, of Tours, who came over with the Conqueror, was their prime founder, and was, no doubt, of the same family as the great saint of that name, whose sister was the mother of St. Patrick. The estate remained in the Martin family until Elizabeth's reign. Nicholas Martin, then the head of this old family, died in 1595 and left four daughters, between whom the estate, and even the house, was divided.

When you visit the church at Puddletown you will notice the tomb of this the last of the Martins of this place. It occupies the south-west corner of the chapel of St. Mary Magdalene, which belongs to Athelhampton, its more common name being the Athelhampton aisle. The beautiful effigies it contains must have been sadly neglected in the past, and their mutilated and defaced condition does not reflect credit upon the successive guardians of the place.

The tomb of Nicholas Martin, with its three monkeys or "martins segeant," bears this epitaph - "Nicholas ye first and Martyn ye last. Good-night, Nicholas" - a no doubt somewhat humorous but surely sad contrast to the pious inscription on the brass to an earlier member of the family. The eldest of the four daughters of this "the last of the Martyns" married a Brune, and soon obtained possession of the most of the other portions of the estate.

On the 11th April the heiress of this "great western family," as it is styled in "The Story of Corfe," became the wife of Sir Ralph Bankes, and in 1665 he sold all the Brune's share in Athelhampton, Burleston, and Southover to Sir Robert Long, of Draycot, Cerne, Wilts. In 1812 the property became vested in the family of the Earl of Mornington by his marriage with Catherine, daughter of Sir James Tylney Long. Their eldest son, fifth Earl of Mornington, great nephew of the great Duke of Wellington, in the year 1848, sold the estate to Mr. George Wood. In 1891 I myself became the owner of the property. You will notice that the estate has only changed hands three times through purchase.

The date of the greater part of the house, as you now see it, is generally assigned to the end of the 15th century. Sir William Martin, who died in 1503, is said to have built the north wing of the courtyard, the beautiful gatehouse, and added a third storey with gables to what, no doubt, was formerly a quadrangular one-storied house, a type so common at the close of the 13th and beginning of the 14th centuries, and which was a style of domestic architecture likely to be resorted to at a period when security was not to be disregarded. As far as I have been able to ascertain, I think there must at one time have been three, if not four, quadrangles or enclosed courts.

The first, outside the gatehouse, extended about as fas as where the present Italian gates stand. This was enclosed on all sides by walls, a church, or more correctly, private chapel, standing in the south-west corner. The second or "fore-court" was enclosed on the N. and E. sides by the mansion, and on the S. and W. by the gatehouse and connecting walls. The third or inner quadrangle was, I believe, surrounded on all sides by different wings of the house. At present only the W. formed by the great hall and S. sides are standing. If there was another quadrangle it would have been where the present modern kitchen offices are.

When one thinks what the house must have been even in the memory of many still living, and sees it in its present mutilated condition, it cannot but fill one with a very deep regret. To me it seems to have been an act of terrible Vandalism to have destroyed so unique and beautiful a specimen of mediaeval domestic architecture as Athelhampton must have been. I believe so lately as the year 1862 the house and quadrangles were practically untouched. But in that year the chapel, gatehouse, enclosing walls of the two front quadrangles, and part of the house were pulled down - the present stables being built from the stones of the gatehouse. The possibility of restoring this gatehouse and forecourt - I do not yet say advisability - has often occurred to me, and any information on the subject I should gladly welcome. You will see a photograph of this beautiful building (taken by Mr. Fane, 1862) in the porch.

On entering the hall you will at once be struck with the beauty of the original open roof with its bold cups, 50ft. in height, ornamented with gilded bosses. This roof was almost white with neglect and mildew when first I saw it, but luckily beyond cleaning and oiling I had to do little to it. I would also draw your attention to the charming oriel window, which forms a connecting passage with the north wing. Notice also the 15th century glass in the east window which faces you on entering.

The rest of the painted windows I have restored, and I was fortunate enough to obtain a complete list of the coats of arms which they formerly contained. You will also remark the beauty of the original carved oak doors, one of which I have been able to put back *in situ*, and the huge wooden bar or bolt, ensconced in one of the fortress-like walls.

The monumental mantlepiece, somewhat French in feeling, of the time of Francois I., bearing the Martin arms and crest (the chains monkey, which you will notice occurs so frequently), I put up a few years ago. I might mention that the letters M.E., which powder the hood of the mantlepiece are not intended to advertise the present owner, but are the initial letters of Sir William Martin and his wife Elizabeth. You will see they occur, too, in the glass in the east window. The linen fold panelling and minstrel gallery are also modern. The old Flemish tapestry was formerly in an old manor house in Oxfordshire.

Passing through the door at the end of the hall under the gallery we enter what was formerly the butlery, plate room, and servant's offices. The first of these rooms, now called the green parlour, I use as a dining room. The green silk which lines the walls is Florentine brocade of the 18th century. All the woodwork and carving in this room was executed by Mr. Parsons, of Dewlish. Notice the arms of Jane Seymour in the south window.

Through the archway in this room we enter the oak parlour. Eight years ago this was the back entrance and scullery. The wainscoting in this room was made from the old oak beams which in nearly every case we had to remove on account of the ends having rotted.

We now pass up the principal staircase, which was put up by Mr. Wood, and constructed by the local carpenter, in place of the original circular stone one. I have not yet touched it. One the first floor you will see the state bedchamber with its original panelling of the time of Henry VII. Notice the curious carved panels in the frieze, the beautiful carved Ham Hill stone mantlepiece, at one time covered over, the oratory, and the washing closet.

Retracting our steps and recrossing the great hall we next enter the north wing. The first room, called the king's ante-room is wainscoted in original panelling of a beautiful dark colour. Notice the original painted glass in the window, and the low stone archway, at one time admitting to the cellars. You will see the sides have been cut away to allow barrels to pass through.

Over this cellar there was formerly the "solar" or ladies' with-drawing room. Traces of the window overlooking the daïs in the hall are still visible.

We next enter the great parlour, a beautifully-proportioned room, with a large high-light mullioned window, divided by a transom, at one end. This room, though somewhat overcrowded with furniture, is at present untouched in the way of decoration. You will see a portion of a dress worn by Queen Elizabeth.

We now ascend the "King's Way," a most interesting stone and oak spiral staircase. The blocks of solid oak which form the upper portion terminate in a newel post, and do not rest on each other as they do in a somewhat similar staircase in the gatehouse at Wolfeton House, Dorchester. From the half landing of this stair, or "way," we enter the long gallery or library. This interior I took upon myself to more or less create; formerly it was divided into three rooms, with a communicating passage running along one side.

The enriched moulded plaster ceiling and panelling are therefore modern. You

will notice a secret staircase in this room, hidden in the thickness of the wall. A pair of boots worn by King Charles I. when a boy are preserved in this room; also a very fine first folio Shakespeare. If I have said little of the contents of the house, its decoration, furniture, and the many objects of interest it contains I am sure you will forgive me, for I fear I have already taken up too much of your time. I must not, however, fail to draw your attention to the old "culver," or pigeon house, in itself sufficiently interesting, but doubly so containing as it does the original "potence," or internal revolving ladder - a thing, I believe, almost unique.

In conclusion I must say a word as to the gardens. The walls and two terraces of Ham Hill stone were begun in 1891, and, incredible as it may seem, some forty thousand tons of stone were used in their construction. The site was formally occupied by cowsheds and dilapidated outbuildings.

The ground then surrounding the house was about three feet higher than its present level, and the former owner told me it was no unusual thing in stormy weather to be called up in the middle of the night to assist in baling the water out of the hall. This, I am happy to say, I have been able to completely remedy.

To the garden, or south, front of the house, you will notice I have added a new gable and turret, corresponding with the old one on the opposite side. This is practically the only new building that has so far been completed. Of its fitness I must leave you to judge. Eight years ago, I found Athelhampton neglected, sadly ill-used, and, may I say, hardly known. Since then I have restored and altered much. If I have made mistakes I trust they are not such as cannot be corrected, and I would ask you in making your criticism to bear in mind that the house, gardens, and surroundings generally are still in a very unfinished state.

Alfred Cart de Lafontaine

A note about the author

Alfred Cart was born in St Pancras, London in 1866, to father Henry Phillipe Cart, a Swiss émigré, and mother Emma. By the 1870s the family were living in a newly built town house in Hampstead, part of the rapidly expanding suburbs of London.

Through the 1870s the household consisted of Alfred, his parents and elder brother, Henry Thomas, and living with them were their household staff Amelia & Fanny. In 1882 Henry Thomas married in Plymouth, and several years later Alfred's nieces and nephews joined the family.

Alfred followed in his brother's footsteps, by attending Balliol College, Oxford from 1885, but in 1887 he left. He doesn't appear to have graduated and in the same year the family changed their name, the Cart family became Cart De Lafontaine, the reason is unknown.

Just 4 years later, in 1891 Alfred Cart de Lafontaine arrived at Athelhampton, he had bought the Manor House and part of the Home Farm. He was just 25 years of age, and appeared fabulously wealthy, there are no clues of how he financed his life style.

He divided his time between London, where he led a bachelor's lifestyle. He lived in his apartment in Mayfair, and on one occasion he listed his residential address as the White's Club, the fine gentleman's club, that continues to this day in London.

Amelia Arnold, his housekeeper, who had served the family for over 20 years, joined Alfred in Dorset and managed the house through what can only have been challenging times, as the house was restored and the gardens were created.

The Author Thomas Hardy, who had known Athelhampton since a child, became an acquaintance of Alfred and a regular visitor. Constance, Alfred's eldest niece, re-told the story in a letter, of a visit to her uncle and enjoying an afternoon tea with him and Mr Hardy.

On a fateful summer evening in 1914, Hardy visited Athelhampton for dinner, and during that evening, the diners learnt that war with Germany had been declared. The discussion at the table led to a view that it would be a short 'affair', however Hardy feared the worse.

Two years of conflict later, Hardy's fears were brought home to Athelhampton. Alfred's youngest nephew was killed at the Battle of the

Somme. The news was devastating, Alfred now aged 52 and unmarried had favoured the nephew and his wife as his heirs.

Alfred left Athelhampton in 1916, and advertised the house, contents and its antiquities for sale. In 1919 after a few years of decline Mr & Mrs George Cochrane purchased Athelhampton. Alfred never returned in his lifetime.

In 1921, Alfred purchased a modest timber framed Tudor house called Aubyns, in Writtle Green near Chelmsford. Alfred became part of village life, but in 1934 a fire destroyed most of the house, Alfred was rescued from the flames, but his housekeeper did not survive.

Until the Second World War, Alfred lived a quieter life in London, then aged in his 80s he was evacuated to Worcester, where he died in 1944. According to his wishes he is buried in the Athelhampton churchyard.

Of Alfred's two nieces, Constance became a teacher and Marie a midwife. The remaining nephew Henry P L Cart De Lafontaine, became a renowned architect. None of the family ever married, in 1982 the last of the Cart De Lafontaine family, Marie, died aged 91.

A list of photographs.